Amazing Birds Story Books For Kids

LAKSHMAN CHAKRABORTY

Published by LAKSHMAN CHAKRABORTY, 2023.

AMAZING BIRDS STORY BOOKS FOR KIDS

First edition. August 26, 2023.

Copyright © 2023 LAKSHMAN CHAKRABORTY.

ISBN: 979-8223703761

Written by LAKSHMAN CHAKRABORTY.

"Flutter the Friendly Finch"

Once upon a time in the green forest lived a little finch named Flutter. Flutter had bright feathers that were as bright as the colors of the rainbow. He lived in a comfortable house on top of a tall tree. Her days were filled with joyful singing and exploring the world around her.

Flutter was not just any finch; He was known throughout the forest as a friendly bird. He greeted each creature with a joyful shout and a warm smile. His friendly nature made him a favorite among all animals.

One sunny morning, Flutter wakes up early, excited to start her day. He welcomed the new day with wings and sang songs of joy. As he flew away, he noticed his friend Rusty, the rabbit, sipping on some sweet clover.

"Good morning, Rusty!" flutter trilled Rusty looked up, his big ears twitching in surprise.

"Good morning, Flutter! You're always so funny," Rusty smiled. Flutter went down to join Rusty. "It's a beautiful day, and I can't help being happy!"

As he spoke, he heard a soft cry from behind the bushes. They peeked through the leaves and saw Penny, the hedgehog, looking very sad.

"What's wrong, Penny?" Flutter asked softly.

Penny wiped away the tears with her little feet. "I've lost my favorite shiny pebble. It's gone, and I can't find it anywhere."

Fluttershy's eyes lit up with determination. "Don't worry, Penny. We'll help you find it!"

And so, Fluttershy, Rusty and Penny start looking for the missing pebble. They checked under leaves, around rocks and even in streams. Flutter's sharp eyes glimpsed under a bush. It was penny pebbles!

Penny's face lit up as she held the pebble in her paws. "Thank you so much, Flutter and Rusty! You're the best friends ever!"

Fuzzy saliva, his feathers swelled with pride. "We're glad we could help, Penny."

Word of Flutter, Rusty, and Penny's kindness spread quickly. The other animals began to see how friendly and helpful Flutter was. Screaming Squirrel asked for help finding acorns and Bear needed help with his beehive.

Flutter didn't hesitate to lend her wings. He showed that being friendly and helpful made the forest a better place for everyone. As the days turned into weeks, Flutter's kindness inspired everyone. The forest becomes a happy and harmonious place, thanks to the friendly finches. His song resonates from tree to tree, fills the air with joy.

And so, Flutter the Friendly Finch continues to spread her warmth and kindness, proving that a little friendship can make the world a brighter and happier place for everyone.

And they all lived forever.

2.
"Waddle's Big Adventure"

Once upon a time, in a peaceful little pond surrounded by tall reeds and colorful flowers, lived a young and curious duck named Waddle. Waddle was no ordinary duck. He had big dreams and a heart full of curiosity that led him on exciting adventures.

One sunny morning, Waddell was swimming in the pond when he noticed a shiny object near the shore. It was a glittering pebble that shone like a star. Waddell's eyes widened in surprise, and he jumped to investigate.

"How wonderful!" He shuddered in surprise. "This is the most beautiful pebble I have ever seen!"

Waddell decided to show his discovery to his friends, Quack and Flap, two other ducks who were known for their adventures. The quack had a bright orange beak, and the softest flap feathers in all the ponds.

Excitedly, Waddle showed them the shiny pebbles. "Look what I got!" She was startled.

Quack and Flap are very surprised. "That's incredible, Waddle!" Quack quacked. "But do you know where this pebble came from?"

Waddle moved. "Not sure, but I think it must be a magical pebble from a distant land!"

Flap her wings flutter and giggle. "Magic or not, it sure is beautiful!"

The three friends decide to embark on a journey to learn more about the origin of pebbles. They wandered by ponds, past rippling reeds and hopping frogs, and into a green forest. As they went deeper, they met a wise old turtle named Turtle.

The turtle looked at the pebbles and smiled. "Ah, young explorers! That pebble is really special. It's part of the Rainbow Rock collection that comes from a hidden cave on the other side of the mountain."

Waddle's eyes sparkled with excitement. "Can you show us the way, Turtle?"

Turtle nodded slowly. "But beware, my young friends, for the journey is not easy. You will face challenges and trials along the way."

Undeterred, Waddle, Quack, and Flap thank Turtle and set off on their big adventure. They climbed mountains, waded across rivers, and even danced in the rain. Each challenge brings them closer to the hidden cave.

Finally, after many days of walking and singing, they reached the cave entrance. Inside, the walls sparkle with colored gems that match the hue of the pebbles. Waddell picked up another pebble, this time a bright blue, and handed it to Flap.

"These pebbles are like treasure," Waddle said. "They remind us that every journey is worth the effort."

As they made their way home, the three friends shared their stories and laughter. The pebbles they found were a sign of their bravery and friendship.

When they return to the pond, they display their pebbles for all to see. The other animals were amazed by their stories and beautiful pebbles. And from that day on, Waddle, Quack and Flap were known as the pond's most daring adventurers.

And so, the story of Waddle's Big Adventure spread across the country, inspiring other curious creatures to explore, discover and create their own stories.

And they all lived happily ever after, sharing their adventures and treasures, just like Waddle and his friends.

the end

3.
"The Curious Case of Chirpy the Chickadee"

Once upon a time, in a colorful forest full of tall trees and buzzing insects, there lived a little bird named Chirpi. Chirpy was a cheerful and curious chickadee who loved to explore the world around him. His feathers are black as coal and his little belly is soft white. Chirpy was known throughout the forest for his melodious songs that could make even the meanest creatures laugh.

One bright morning, Chirpy woke up with a special feeling in her tiny heart. He heard the story of a magical golden seed hidden deep in the forest. This seed was asked to grant a single wish to whoever found it. Chirpy's eyes sparkled with excitement as he decided to embark on a great adventure to find the legendary seed.

Spreading his little wings, Chirpy flew through the trees, leaping from branch to branch and singing his happy song. Along the way, he met his friends: Sammy the Squirrel, Bonnie the Bunny and

Freddy the Frog. He tells them about his quest to find the magical golden seed and they decide to join him on his journey.

The forest was full of challenges, but Chirpy and his friends faced them with courage and teamwork. They crossed bubbling brooks over swaying vines and climbed tall trees to glimpse the shimmering sun. Chirpy songs echoed through the forest, lifting their spirits whenever they felt tired.

One day, while they were exploring near a sparkling stream, they came across an unusual tree whose leaves glowed like fireflies. At the base of the tree were heaps of sunflower seeds, and among them was a seed that shone like gold. Chirpy's heart raced to recognize it as a magical gold seed!

Amazed, the chirpy gently picked up the golden seed and held it in its tiny beak. He closed his eyes and fulfilled his will with all his might. He wished happiness to fill the forest forever, so that every creature would know the joy he felt when he sang his song.

Suddenly, a warm breeze blew through the forest, accompanied by a soft, rustling sound. When Chirpy opened his eyes, he saw that the forest was bathed in a soft golden light. The flowers bloomed in vivid colors, and even the sad old owl cracked a smile.

Chirpy realized that his wish was fulfilled! The magical golden seed spread happiness throughout the forest, as she had hoped. His friends cheered, and together they celebrated with a joyful chorus of songs that echoed far and wide.

From that day on, Chirpy the Chickadee continued to sing his song, and his cheerful melody carried the magic of the golden seed in every note. He taught all beings that even the smallest of them can make a big difference by spreading happiness and kindness.

And so, the curious case of Chirpy the Chickadee became a legendary story in the forest, inspiring generations of young birds to be brave, curious and kind, just like Chirpy and his friends.

"Rainbow's Quest for Colors"

Once upon a time, in a land of magic and wonder, there lived a little bird named Rainbow. The rainbow was no ordinary bird; He was a special bird with white feathers. He lived on top of a tree, where he could see the whole world below.

One sunny morning, Rainbow looked around and saw all the other birds with their beautiful and vibrant feathers. The red cardinal, the blue jay, the green parrot and the yellow canary - they all had colorful feathers that sparkled like precious gems. Rainbow felt a little sad because her feathers had no color.

One day, Rainbow decided she wanted to find color for her feathers as well. He flapped his wings and set off to discover the mystery of color. He flew through valleys, over mountains and across rivers, meeting various creatures along the way.

First, he met a wise old turtle. "Oh, dear rainbow," said the turtle, "colors come from the heart. They are a reflection of your innermost feelings." Rainbow didn't quite understand, but she thanked the turtle and continued on her way.

Next, he encounters a friendly butterfly. "Hello, Rainbow," the butterfly greeted her. "Colors are all around us, in the flowers, the sky and the water. Just look and you will find them." Rainbow smiled and thanked Butterfly before moving on.

As she travels, Rainbow notices colorful flowers blooming in the field. He landed on a bright red flower, hoping that its color would rub off on him. But no matter how hard he tried, his feathers remained white.

Feeling somewhat disappointed, Rainbow landed near a sparkling river. She looked at her reflection and whispered, "I wish I had colors like the rainbow." Suddenly, the water around him began to sparkle with all the colors of the rainbow. The rainbow wondered that the river had given her colors.

Excited, the rainbow flaunts its colorful feathers and returns home. But when he landed in his tree, the colors began to fade, his feathers turned white again. Rainbow felt sad, thinking that colors were never meant for her.

Just then a gentle breeze rustled his feathers and he heard a soft voice. It was the wind, whispering, "Rainbow, the secret of color lies within you. It's not about the outside, but how you feel inside." Rainbow realized that she had misunderstood the journey. He didn't need colorful feathers to be special. He already had a heart full of kindness and curiosity. With a glad heart, he looked down at the world below and saw beauty in everything - blue skies, green trees, colorful flowers and sparkling rivers.

From that day on, Rainbow embraced her fluffy white feathers and spread happiness wherever she went. He realized that colors are more than what you see; They were passions that make life beautiful.

And so, Rainbow's search for color teaches her the most valuable lesson - that true beauty comes from within, and shines through the way we treat others and the world around us. And whenever he flew across the sky, his feathers shone with all the colors of the rainbow, because his heart was truly colorful and bright.

5.
"Oliver Owl's Moonlight Mystery"

Once upon a time, in a quiet and magical forest, there lived a wise old owl named Oliver. Oliver Owl was known for his large round eyes and his love for exploring mysteries. Every night, as the sun sets and the stars appear in the sky, Oliver wakes up from his cozy tree hollow and spreads his wings.

One clear night, when the moon shone like a silver lantern, Oliver felt a strange excitement in the air. He sensed something different was about to happen. With curiosity in his mind, he flew silently through the trees, his feathers fluttering like a ghost in the night.

As Oliver climbed over the forest, he noticed something sparkling near the pond. It was a shimmering path of light leading into the forest. Oliver's heart races with anticipation and he decides to follow the mysterious path.

The trail wound through the dark trees, and Oliver's sharp eyes saw the blazing fireflies that seemed to guide him. He followed their soft glow until he reached a clearing, where a group of animals gathered around a campfire. There were squirrels, rabbits, and even a friendly fox.

"Welcome, Oliver Owl!" They were singing, their eyes shining with joy.

"Hello, everyone! What brings you all together on this magical night?" Oliver asked.

A wise old rabbit named Rosie came forward and explained, "Oliver, we have a special tradition. Every full moon we get together to share stories, laughter and friendship. We call it the Moon Festival."

Oliver was amazed by their wonderful ideas. He joined the circle, and told each animal story one by one. The squirrel told a story of heroism, the fox shared a story of kindness, and the rabbit told a story of the importance of working together.

When it was Oliver's turn, he told them about the magic of the night sky, how the moon and stars held secrets that only those who believed could understand. The animals listened with wide eyes, fascinated by his words.

As the night darkened, the moonlight bathed the clearing in soft light. Fireflies danced around the creatures, creating a magical scene. And in that moment, Oliver realized that the real secret of the night was the beauty of friendship and the joy of coming together.

The Moonlight Festival continues long into the night, with laughter, stories and shared food. Oliver felt a warmth in his heart that he had never felt before. As the first rays of dawn began to touch the horizon, the animals bid their farewells, promising to meet again at the next full moon.

Oliver Owl returned to his tree hollow, feeling grateful for the wonderful experience. He realized that sometimes, the greatest secrets are not hidden in the shadows, but in the bonds we form with others. And so, Oliver drifted off to sleep, knowing that he had uncovered a moonlight secret that was even more beautiful than he had imagined.

And so, dear friends, remember that the moon and stars hold not only their own secrets, but also the secrets of our hearts when we share them with others. And just like Oliver Owl, you can discover the magic of friendship and the joy of mystery that brings us together under the moonlight.

6.
"Sunny the Singing Sparrow"

Once upon a time there lived a little sparrow named Sunny in a colorful meadow. Sunny was no ordinary sparrow - she had a special gift. He could sing the most beautiful tunes that would make everyone laugh.

Every morning when the sun peeked over the horizon, Sunny would sit on the branch of his favorite tree. She sang her sweet song in a happy heart. His music echoed through the meadow, waking all the other creatures and filling their hearts with happiness.

Sunny's songs were not only beautiful; It was magical. His songs had the power to make flowers bloom, turn gray clouds into fluffy whites and even mend soured friendships.

One day, when Sunny was singing her heart out, a sad butterfly named Bella appeared. Bella lost her way and couldn't find her butterfly friends. He landed on a nearby rock and sighed.

Sunny noticed Bella's distress and flew to her. "Why are you sad?" He cried softly.

Bella looked up, her eyes still full of tears. "I'm lost. I can't find my friends, and I don't know how to get home."

Sunny gave a warm smile. "Don't worry, Bella. I'll help you find your friends." And with that, he sang a soothing melody that carried hope on its wings.

As Sunny sings, the notes dance around Bella, creating a shimmering path in the air. Bela's heart starts to lighten and she follows the path led by Sunny's song.

With each step, Bella's wings grew stronger and her grief began to fade away. He followed the magical music until he found his friends playing near a field of colorful flowers. Bella's heart swelled with joy, and she joined her friends in their playful dance.

Sunny's singing not only brought Bela back to her friends but also brought happiness back to her heart. The other creatures of the meadow gathered around, amazed at the beautiful transformation they had witnessed.

From that day Sunny's singing became more special. He not only brought joy to the meadows but also helped animals in need with his magical tunes. Whenever someone was sad or lost, they knew they could count on Sunny's songs to lift their spirits.

And so, Sunny the Singing Sparrow continues to share her gift with the world, reminding everyone that a little song and a lot of kindness can make even the darkest days brighter. And her meadow was always full of laughter, friendship and the sweet sound of music magic.

And that ends the story of Sunny the Singing Sparrow. Remember, just like Sunny, you have something special inside you that can bring happiness to others too.

7.
"Feathers and Friends: A Tale of Cooperation"

Once upon a time, in a lively forest full of chirping birds, lived a curious little robin named Rosie. Rosie was known for her beautiful red feathers and her cheerful song that echoed through the forest. Rosie loved exploring every corner of the forest and making new friends.

One sunny morning, as Rosie was hopping from branch to branch, she noticed a group of birds gathered around a large tree. There were blue jays, sparrows, finches and even a wise old owl named Oliver. They seem to be having a serious conversation.

Intrigued, Rosie jumped to join them. He greeted everyone with a cheerful tweet, "Hello, friends! What's up?"

Oliver, the wise owl, said softly, "We have a problem, Rosie. Winter is coming, and we must build warm nests to keep us safe and comfortable. But we are all different kinds of birds, and we don't know how to work together."

Rosie looked at her feathered friends and nodded in understanding. He had an idea. "What if we all brought something special from our own habitats to build nests? That way, our nests would be as strong and warm as our friendships!"

The birds looked at each other and smiled, realizing that Rosie's idea was a brilliant one. So, they embark on a mission to collect materials from their various homes.

Rosie collects soft twigs and dry leaves from the ground. Sparrows brought small feathers found near the river. The blue jays, with their strong beaks, came up with strong branches. Even Oliver, the wise owl, contributed some of his feathers for extra warmth.

As they worked together, something wonderful happened. Not only were they building strong and comfortable nests, they were getting to know each other better. They laughed, shared stories and discovered how much they had in common.

Finally, after many days of hard work and many laughs, the nests were ready. Each nest was unique, a mix of different materials that reflected the unity of their friendship. The birds felt proud of what they had done together.

When winter comes, the forest is covered with a soft sheet of snow. Feeling warm and safe, the birds crawl into their nests. Rosie's concept of cooperation not only created strong nests but also forged strong bonds of friendship between the birds.

As the winter days turn to spring, the forest becomes resplendent with the joyous singing of birds. They realized that when they work together and embrace their differences, they can achieve amazing things.

And so, Feathers and Friends becomes a beloved story in the forest, reminding everyone that no matter how different they are, when they cooperate and support each other, they can create something truly beautiful.

And they all lived, chirped and hummed happily.

8.
"Bella the Brave Blue Jay"

Once upon a time, in a peaceful forest, lived Bella, a brave blue Jay. Bella was no ordinary blue jay; He was known for his bravery and courage. His blue feathers sparkle like the sky, and his eyes shine with determination.

One sunny morning, Bella's forest friends gathered for a picnic near the old oak tree. Bella loved spending time with her friends, sharing stories and laughter. But something was different that day. A shadow passed over the picnic spot, and everyone saw a group of mischievous squirrels, led by Squawky, the loudest squirrel among them all.

Squeaky pointed to the juicy berries that Bella's friends had brought for the picnic. "These berries look delicious," he exclaimed, "let's eat some!"

Bella, ever alert, noticed that her friends were getting worried. Squeaky's gang had a reputation for causing trouble. Bella knew she had to step up.

Her heart beating fast, Bella flapped her wings and perched on a branch above the picnic. "Hey, scream!" He called out, his voice clear and confident.

He looked surprised. "Well, well, if Bella isn't Brave Blue Jay. What do you want, Bella?"

Bella puffed out her chest and replied, "We're all here to have a peaceful picnic. We can share the berries, but let's not take more than our fair share."

Squeaky's gang laughed and started picking berries anyway. Bella's friends looked worried, but Bella wasn't about to back down.

He swooped and landed right in front of Squeaky. "Stop! These berries are for everyone. If we share, there's plenty for everyone." yelled and wagged his tail, clearly annoyed. "And what will you do if we don't listen?"

Bella looked around at her friends, and then back at Squawky. "I'll call for the wise old owl," he announced.

Squeaky's bravery fails. The Wise Old Owl was known for his wisdom and fairness. Bella played her trump card.

Squeaky's team inadvertently returns the extra berries and Bella's friends breathe a sigh of relief. The picnic continues peacefully, with everyone enjoying the delicious berries and each other's company.

After the picnic, Bella's friends gathered around her, impressed by her bravery. "You're amazing, Bella," chirped Sammy the squirrel. "Yeah, you stand up to Squeaky and his gang," Lily Rabbit added.

Bella smiled, proud of what she had done. "Sometimes, it takes a little courage to stand up for what's right."

And since that day Bella Bella, known as the Brave Blue Jay, is a true hero of the forest. He taught his friends that bravery is not about being big or strong, but about standing up for what is just and right.

And so, Bella's story of courage spreads throughout the forest, inspiring all her animals to be just as brave and kind as their brave blue Jay friend.

And they all lived happily and peacefully.

The End

9.

"Tilly and the Talking Toucan"

Once upon a time, in a peaceful forest, lived Bella, a brave blue Jay. Bella was no ordinary blue jay; He was known for his bravery and courage. His blue feathers sparkle like the sky, and his eyes shine with determination.

One sunny morning, Bella's forest friends gathered for a picnic near the old oak tree. Bella loved spending time with her friends, sharing stories and laughter. But something was different that day. A shadow passed over the picnic spot, and everyone saw a group of mischievous squirrels, led by Squawky, the loudest squirrel among them all.

Squeaky pointed to the juicy berries that Bella's friends had brought for the picnic. "These berries look delicious," he exclaimed, "let's eat some!"

Bella, ever alert, noticed that her friends were getting worried. Squeaky's gang had a reputation for causing trouble. Bella knew she had to step up.

Her heart beating fast, Bella flapped her wings and perched on a branch above the picnic. "Hey, scream!" He called out, his voice clear and confident.

He looked surprised. "Well, well, if Bella isn't Brave Blue Jay. What do you want, Bella?"

Bella puffed out her chest and replied, "We're all here to have a peaceful picnic. We can share the berries, but let's not take more than our fair share."

Squeaky's gang laughed and started picking berries anyway. Bella's friends looked worried, but Bella wasn't about to back down.

He swooped and landed right in front of Squeaky. "Stop! These berries are for everyone. If we share, there's plenty for everyone."

yelled and wagged his tail, clearly annoyed. "And what will you do if we don't listen?"

Bella looked around at her friends, and then back at Squawky. "I'll call for the wise old owl," he announced.

Squeaky's bravery fails. The Wise Old Owl was known for his wisdom and fairness. Bella played her trump card.

Squeaky's team inadvertently returns the extra berries and Bella's friends breathe a sigh of relief. The picnic continues peacefully, with everyone enjoying the delicious berries and each other's company.

After the picnic, Bella's friends gathered around her, impressed by her bravery. "You're amazing, Bella," chirped Sammy the squirrel.

"Yeah, you stand up to Squeaky and his gang," Lily Rabbit added. Bella smiled, proud of what she had done. "Sometimes, it takes a little courage to stand up for what's right."

And since that day Bella Bella, known as the Brave Blue Jay, is a true hero of the forest. He taught his friends that bravery is not about being big or strong, but about standing up for what is just and right.

And so, Bella's story of courage spreads throughout the forest, inspiring all her animals to be just as brave and kind as their brave blue Jay friend.

And they all lived happily and peacefully.

The End

10.
"Peep's Great Migration"

Once upon a time, in a cozy little forest, lived Pip, a small and cheerful bird. Pip was a curious little bird with bright orange feathers and an adventurous heart. Pip the bird lived with a large flock of friends who loved to play and sing together.

One day, as the leaves began to change color and the air cooled, Pip noticed something else. The wind seemed to carry whispers of change, and the older birds spoke of a great journey called "migration." Migration means traveling to warmer places when winter comes.

Pip was excited about this new adventure, but there was a problem. Peep was afraid to fly too far and leave the cozy forest home. Pip's friend, Waddle the Wise Duck, notices Pip's anxiety and offers some advice. "Pip," Waddle said gently, "immigration may seem scary, but it's a chance to see new places and make new friends. You won't be alone - we'll all be together!"

Pip's heart lightened at Waddell's encouragement. Pip started preparing for the journey. Collecting feathers, packing a small bag and saying goodbye to the forest were all part of the exciting process. The forest hummed with excitement as the sails were readied.

The morning of migration had arrived, and the sky was painted in shades of pink and gold. Peeping hearts flutter like wings. "Are you ready, Pip?" Chirping sound

Peep nodded, and with a deep breath the journey began. The wind carried them over the trees, and Pip marveled at the vast sky. The clouds looked like fluffy pillows, and the sun warmed their feathers. Days turned into weeks as flocks of sheep rose over hills, rivers and fields. Pip makes new friends with far-flung birds, such as chatty blue jays and colorful cardinals. Each day was a new adventure, and Pip felt the fear disappear.

One evening, as they rested on a swaying branch, Pip realized something amazing. The journey turned out to be more than just a migration – it was a great story of courage, friendship and discovery. Peeping's heart swelled with happiness.

As winter approached, the herd found a warm and comfortable place to stay. Peeked out as snowflakes gently covered the ground and stars twinkled in the sky. It was a magical sight that Pip would never forget.

Spring is back, and with it the desire to return home. Pip's heart was full, knowing the journey back would be just as incredible. With new confidence, Pip and the flock spread their wings and headed back into the forest.

Back home, the forest welcomes them with open arms. Pip felt a deep sense of belonging, knowing that the journey had changed them all in beautiful ways. Pip's friends gathered around to hear the stories of their travels, and Pip's stories filled the air with wonder. And so, Pip's Great Migration became a story shared by generations of birds. The forest echoes with laughter, friendship and reminders that even the tiniest of birds can find the courage to embark on the greatest journey.

And this is the story of Pip, the brave little bird who discovers that sometimes, the greatest adventures come from flying outside of our comfort zone.

the end

11.
"Robin's Egg Rescue"

Once upon a time, in a cozy little forest, there lived a chirpy and cheerful robin named Ruby. Ruby had bright red feathers that sparkled like ruby gems in the sunlight. He was known for his beautiful song that echoed through the trees every morning.

One sunny morning, while Ruby was singing her sweet melody, she noticed a small blue egg in a nest on a tree. The house belonged to her friend Rosie Robin. But Rosie was nowhere to be seen. Ruby knew something was wrong.

Curious and anxious, Ruby hopped over to the nest and peered inside. There, he saw a single, delicate blue egg. It was so beautiful and delicate that Ruby couldn't believe her eyes. He knew he had to protect it.

Just as Ruby was about to call for help, she heard a faint noise nearby. It was Rusty the Raccoon, a mischievous forest creature known for his trouble-making ways. Ruby knew she had to act fast. "Hey, Rusty!" Ruby screamed loudly. "What are you doing here?" Rusty peeked out from behind a bush, looking a little guilty. "Oh, hi, Ruby. Just exploring, you know."

Ruby knew that rust was not good. "Well, I see you're hanging around Rosie's nest. But don't you know that this egg needs to be protected? It's Rosie's precious egg!"

Rusty's eyes widened as he realized what he had stumbled upon. "Oh, I didn't know that. I promise, I won't touch it."

Ruby knew she couldn't trust Rusty completely. He decided to keep an eye on her, just in case. "I appreciate it, Rusty. But I'll be here to make sure nothing happens to this egg. Rosie will be back soon."

Days turned to night, and Ruby bravely guarded the egg. He sang praises to keep the egg warm and safe. Rust, surprisingly, stayed away, watching from afar as Ruby fulfilled her promise.

One beautiful morning, Rosie returned to her home. She went out in search of food to nourish her eggs. Ruby was glad to see her friend back. "Rosie, I was watching over your egg while you were gone. I knew it was important to keep it safe."

Tears of gratitude welled up in Rosie's eyes as she looked at Ruby. "Thank you, Ruby. You are a true friend."

Just then, a small crack appeared in the egg shell. Rosie and Ruby looked on with a small pout in anticipation. A baby robin was laying eggs! It was a magical moment they shared together.

As days passed, the baby robin grew stronger and fluffier. Rosie and Ruby took turns caring for the little one, teaching him to sing and fly. Rusty, who was touched by Ruby's kindness, even offered to help gather food for the growing family.

And so, in the heart of the forest, a beautiful bond was formed between a brave robin, a worried raccoon and a loving mother.

Ruby's dedication to protecting the robin's egg not only saved a life but also brought together unlikely friends.

the end

Moral of the story: Friends help and protect each other, even when it's not easy.

12.

"The Magical Melodies of Melody the Mockingbird"

Once upon a time, in a lush and vibrant forest, there lived a cheerful little mockingbird named Melody. Melody was no ordinary bird; He had a special gift. He could imitate the songs of all the other birds in the forest.

Every morning, as the sun peeked through the leaves, Melody would sit on her favorite branch and begin her act. He began with a sweet robin's song, then smoothly transitioned into a canary's flute-like trill. Other birds will gather around in awe of his genius.

Melody loved sharing her gifts, but deep inside, she felt a little lonely. He wished he could sing his own song, a tune that was uniquely his. One day he saw a group of colorful butterflies dancing in the air. Inspired by their grace, he decided to create a tune that captured the beauty of the forest.

He spent the day listening to thundering streams, rustling leaves and distant rumbles of thunder. He mixed these words with the joy of his own heart and soon, he composed the most charming melody.

When Melody sang her new song for the first time, the entire forest fell silent. His music was a mixture of the wonders of nature and his own feelings, and it filled the air with magic. Other birds join in, adding their own tunes to the melody. It was a symphony of unity and harmony.

As Melody's song spread throughout the forest, something wonderful happened. Animals came from far and wide to listen. Squirrels, rabbits and even a wise old owl gathered to enjoy the magical tunes. Melody's heart swelled with joy as she realized her gift wasn't just about copying—it was about bringing everyone together.

The melody of the melody reached the people of the nearby villages. They came to the forest with a smile. They danced with the animals and listened to sweet sounds, feeling the connection between themselves, nature and each other.

Since that day, Melody continues to sing her magical tunes, but now, she incorporates her own unique song into each performance. The forest became a place of joy and friendship, where small and large animals, with different songs and sounds, came together in perfect harmony.

And so, the story of Melody the Mockingbird and her magical tune became legendary in the forest. The memories of her songs and the love she shared lived on, creating a bond between all creatures that lasted generations.

And that, dear children, is how Melody the Mockingbird's gift of music has brought everyone together and made the forest a truly magical place where every note carries the essence of unity and love.

13.
Leo's Sky-High Dreams

Once upon a time, in a cozy nest atop a tall tree, lived a little blue bird named Leo. Leo had big dreams as big as the open sky. Every day, he saw other birds flying in the air and he wanted with all his heart to join them in the bright blue sky.

Leo spent his days hovering around tree branches, practicing his take-offs and landings. He listened attentively to the songs of the wind and the whispers of the clouds, hoping to learn their secrets. But no matter how hard he tries, Leo can't seem to fly more than short distances.

One sunny morning, Leo sat on a branch, feeling a little down. His friend, a wise old owl named Oliver, noticed Leo's distress. With a gentle thud, Oliver landed next to Leo.

"Hello, Leo. Does today seem to be bothering you?" Oliver asked, his eyes shining softly.

Leo sighed. "I see other birds flying so high, and I want to join them. But no matter how much I practice, I can't fly very high."

Oliver smiled kindly. "Ah, Leo, did you know that every bird is different? Just because you can't fly like others doesn't mean you can't touch the sky in your own way."

Leo blinked, curious. "What do you mean, Oliver?"

Oliver spread his wings and lifted off the branch. "Close your eyes, Leo, and listen to the wind."

Leo closed his eyes and listened intently. He felt the wind brush against his feathers, whispering secrets to him. He opened his eyes, inspired.

"I may not fly very far, but I can dance with the wind!" Leo shouted.

Oliver shook his head. "Well, Leo. You have a gift for dancing with the wind, painting the sky with your beautiful moves."

From that day on, Leo embraced his special talents. He would leap from branch to branch and catch the whisper of the wind and move like a leaf in the wind. The other birds watched Leo's joyful dance in awe.

One evening, as the sun began to set and paint the sky orange and pink, Leo's fellow birds gathered around him.

"Leo, your dances are like magic," Bella shouted to the blue joy.

"We've never seen anything so beautiful," Sunny Sparrow tweeted.

Leo blushed and thanked his friends. With their encouragement, Leo's dance becomes more mesmerizing and soon, word of his graceful performance spreads throughout the forest.

One day, during a great gathering of forest animals, Leo stood on the edge of a high mountain. His heart was racing, but his dream gave him courage. Taking a deep breath, Leo leapt into the air, catching the air with his outstretched wings. She danced higher and higher, leaving a trail of beauty against the blue sky.

The forest animals looked on in awe as Leo painted the sky with his dance. He whirled, whirled and whirled through the air, his dreams taking him higher than he could have imagined.

When Leo finally returned to the ground, the applause was thunderous. Leo's eyes sparkled with joy as he realized that he had achieved his dream, not by flying away, but by dancing with the wind.

Leo's sky-high dreams came true in the most magical and unexpected way. And from that day, whenever a gentle breeze rustled the leaves and the sun sank below the horizon, Leo's graceful dance would fill the sky, reminding everyone that dreams can be as limitless as the sky.

And so, Leo's story taught all the animals in the forest that we each have a unique gift and that by embracing our own talents we can touch the sky in our own way.

14.
"Flora the Fearless Flamingo"

Once upon a time, in a land full of sparkling lakes and tall palm trees, there lived a flamingo named Flora. Flora was no ordinary flamingo - she was widely known as "Flora the Fearless". Why? For he was never afraid of anything, not even something that ruffled the feathers of his friends in worry.

Flora had the pinkest feathers you can imagine and her legs were long and beautiful. She loved to stand on one leg by the sparkling lake, balancing like a ballerina. But Flora wasn't just beautiful; He was curious. He wanted to explore every corner of their colorful world.

One sunny morning, when the water glistened in golden sunlight, Flora gathered her friends - Freddy the Frog, Bella the Butterfly and Remy the Rabbit. "Let's go on an adventure!" He chirped "There's a hidden island across the lake, and I want to see what's there."

Freddy the Frog gurgles. "But Flora, the water can be deep and scary."

Flora laughed, shaking her head. "Don't worry, Freddy. I've swam in deep water before. I'll be right here with you."

Bella the butterfly flapped her wings nervously. "What if there are big birds who don't like visitors?"

Flora winked. "I'll use my friendly charm, and we'll make new friends together."

Remy Rabbit snorted. "And if we get lost?"

Flora smiled. "No chance! I have an excellent sense of direction."

With Flora's fearless confidence, her friends agreed to the adventure. They waded into the water, Flora leading the way. As they swam across the sparkling lake, Freddy, Bella, and Remy noticed how the water felt cooler and deeper. But Flora stayed with them, making sure they were safe.

Finally, they reach the secret island. To their surprise, it was like stepping into a magical garden, filled with colorful flowers and friendly birds of all sizes. Flora greeted the new friends with her warm smile and soon everyone was laughing and playing together.

Flora showed Freddie how to jump from a lily pad, Bella how to scurry between flowers, and Remy how to jump for joy. New friends were amazed by Flora's fearlessness and kindness.

As the sun began to set, casting a warm orange glow across the sky, Flora's friends gathered around her. "Flora," Freddy said, "we were scared at first, but you've shown us that being brave doesn't mean you're never afraid. It means facing your fears and finding fun on the other side."

Flora beamed. "That's right, my friends. Being fearless doesn't mean you're never afraid—it just means you don't let fear stop you from discovering new wonders."

With hearts full of courage, Flora and her friends vowed to explore more hidden places and make more friends. And as they headed home, they knew that with Flora the Fearless Flamingo by their side, they could conquer any adventure, big or small.

And so, Flora's fearless spirit inspired everyone she met, showing them that a little courage can lead to the most magical discoveries.

the end

15.

"Flora the Fearless Flamingo"

Once upon a time, in a lively and bustling swamp, there lived a little flamingo named Flora. Flora was different from the other flamingos in the flock. While her feathered friends were content with their daily routine, Flora had a curiosity and a desire for adventure.

Flora's feathers were a bright shade of pink, and her long legs were perfect for walking in shallow water. But what sets Flora apart the most is her spirit. He was fearless, always looking for new places to explore and new friends to meet.

One sunny morning, as the sun's golden rays danced over the water, Flora decided it was time for a great adventure. He waved his wings to his friends and began his journey.

As she ventures beyond her familiar swamp, Flora discovers a dense and mysterious forest. Tall trees stretched skyward, their leaves whispering secrets to the wind. Flora's heart raced with excitement as she stepped into the shade of the tree.

In the heart of the forest, Flora meets Benny, a mischievous squirrel with unblinking eyes. Benny showed Flora how to swing from vines and balance on branches. Flora laughed so hard that the forest echoed with her joy. She made a new friend who was just as fearless as she was.

One day, while Flora and Benny are exploring, they hear a faint cry for help. After the sound, they discover a small bird clutching a bunch of grapes. Flora's fearless heart led her to help the bird, carefully freeing the vines until the little creature was free.

The grateful bird introduces herself as Lola, a colorful canary who has lost her way. Flora and Benny comfort Lola and assure her that they will help her find her way back home.

Together, the trio embarked on a new adventure - a journey through the forest, across the meadows and over the mountains. Along the way, they encounter challenges and surprises, but Flora's fearlessness and her friends' tenacity carry them forward.

After many days of travel, they reached a familiar swamp and Lola's joy knew no bounds. Flora, Benny and Lola became an inseparable team, each bringing their unique strengths to the group.

As the seasons changed and time passed, Flora's bravery and friendship transformed the swamps and forests into places where all creatures, great and small, lived together in harmony. Flora's fearless spirit created a bond that connected them all.

And so, Flora the Fearless Flamingo, Benny the Brave Squirrel and Lola the Lively Canary continue to explore and spread their message of friendship and fearlessness. They taught everyone they met that with courage and a caring heart, anything was possible.

And to this day, the swamps and forests echo with laughter, the vibrant colors of friendship and the memory of Flora, the flamingo who showed the world that being fearless can bring magic to even the most ordinary day.

16.
"Whisper the Woodpecker's Woodland Whimsy"

Once upon a time, in a peaceful forest, there lived a little woodpecker named Whisper. The whispers were no ordinary woodpeckers; He had a special gift. He could talk to all the creatures of the forest, from the tiniest ant to the tallest tree.

Whisper had a cozy nest atop a tall oak tree. Every morning, he would wake up with the first rays of the sun and gently knock on the tree to say hello to his fellow creatures. Squirrels, rabbits, and even the wise old owl would gather to listen to his stories.

One bright morning, while Whisper was tapping his tree in a gentle rhythm, a worried chipmunk named Chippy ran up to him. "Whisper, you must help us," cried Chippy. "The berries we eat have disappeared from our usual place. We're hungry!" Whisper nodded and promised to investigate. He spread his wings and flew across the forest, talking to various animals and asking if they had seen anything unusual. Along the way, he talks to Ricky the rabbit, Hootie the owl, and Sammy the squirrel. But no one had any idea about the missing berries.

Just as Whisper was about to give up, he heard a soft chuckle from a nearby bush. He peeked through the leaves and saw the mischievous raccoon twins, Rocky and Remy. They rolled the berries down a hill, laughing all the while.

Whisper flew up and landed on a nearby branch. "Hey, Rocky and Remy," he said with a smile. "Why are you taking all the berries?" Rocky looked sheepish, and Remy frowned. "We were just playing," admitted Rocky. "We didn't know that animals needed them to eat."

Whisper explained to the raccoon twins about the importance of sharing and how their actions were affecting other animals. Rocky and Remy apologize for their mistake and promise to make things right.

Under Whisper's guidance, they gathered all the berries they had taken and placed them in their proper place. The other animals watched as the berries reappeared, and they cheered for Rocky and Remy's change of heart.

As a sign of their friendship and to remind everyone of the value of sharing, Whisper suggests that the woodland creatures hold a berry feast together. Everyone came up with something special, whether it was nuts, fruit or delicious mushrooms. Under the shade of an oak tree they held a sumptuous feast, sharing whispering stories that made everyone laugh.

From that day on, the woodland creatures became even closer friends. They realized that thinking of others and taking care of the forest called them all home. Rocky and Remy, with Whisper's guidance, become guardians of sharing, making sure no one goes hungry again.

And so, Whisper the Woodpecker's woodland whimsy brought joy, togetherness and friendship to the forest, reminding everyone that even the smallest acts of kindness can make a big difference.

the end

17.
"Skye and the Lost Starling"

Once upon a time in the peaceful land of Aviania, where birds of all colors and sizes lived together, there lived a young bird named Sky. Skye was a brave and curious little sparrow with feathers as blue as the sky. He had a keen eye for adventure and mystery.

One sunny morning, as Skye wandered near the Whispering Woods, she heard a soft, melodious chirping. After the magical sound, he discovered a tiny star sitting on a branch. The star's feathers shone like stars in the night, and its song was like a magical melody that filled the air.

Skye introduced herself, and Starling told her that it was lost and couldn't find its way back to her flock. Its name was Twinkle, and it was separated from its family during a sudden gust of wind. Skye's heart swelled with sympathy for the lost little stars. "Don't worry, Twinkle. I'll help you find your family," she chirped with determination.

Together, Skye and Twinkle set off on a grand adventure across Aviania. They flew over rolling hills, through colorful meadows and even over sparkling rivers. Along the way, they encounter a friendly owl who guides them and a group of cheerful robins who share their food.

As the day turned into night, Skye and Twinkle's friendship grew stronger. They shared stories, laughed and sang, making their own joyful melodies. Skye's determination and Twinkle's courage inspired them to keep going, no matter how vast and unfamiliar the world seemed.

One evening, as they reached the edge of the Whispering Woods, they heard a familiar chirping in the distance. Twinkle's eyes lit up as she recognized her family's voice. With renewed energy, Skye and Twinkle followed the sweet sounds until they emerged into a clearing bathed in moonlight.

There, under the blazing stars, Twinkle was happily reunited with her family. The starling parents embraced their lost little one with tears of joy, and the entire flock welcomed Skye with open wings for her kindness and bravery.

As a token of gratitude, the stars taught Skye a special song filled with all the love and happiness they felt. Skye's heart swelled as she learned the beautiful tune, and she realized that this adventure had not only brought Twinkle back to her family, but also a new song to share with her friends in Avinia.

With a fond farewell, Skye and Twinkle return to their respective homes carrying memories of their incredible trip. From that day forward, whenever the sky sang the starling's song, the entire land of Aviania would join in, creating a symphony of unity and friendship that would echo across the skies.

And so, the story of Skye and the Lost Starling has become an avian legend, reminding everyone that kindness, courage and friendship in the face of challenges can light up dark skies and bring joy to all.

the end

18.

"Penny and the Precious Pelican"

Once upon a time, in a sunny seaside village, there lived a curious little girl named Penny. Penny loved exploring the beach and watching the waves dance to the ocean breeze. But there was one animal Penny was always excited to see: Percy, the precious pelican. Percy was no ordinary pelican. He had feathers as white as clouds and a beak that shone like polished silver. His heart was as big as the ocean and his love for shiny things shone like the stars in the sky. Penny and Percy become best friends. Every morning, Penny would walk the shore with small bags of shiny seashells and colorful pebbles. Percy would jump at him, flapping his wings in glee. Penny would giggle, "Percy, my dear friend, I've brought you some treasure!"

Percy carefully picked up each shiny gift with his lips and carried it to a secret place near his nest. She cherished these gifts, because they made her feel special and loved.

One day a storm arose from the sea. Dark clouds covered the sky, and the waves grew wild and terrifying. Penny worries about Percy, knowing he might get into trouble. He put on his raincoat, grabbed his umbrella and ran to the beach.

When Penny arrived, she saw Percy sitting on a rock, struggling to stay still against the strong wind. She called out to him, "Percy, hold on! I'm coming!"

Penny jumped into the water, her rain boots splashing in the waves. With each step, the water grew deeper, and his heart raced. Finally, he reached Percy and held out his hand. Percy spread his wings and jumped into Penny's outstretched arms.

With great determination, Penny returns to shore with Percy to safety. He knew he had to find a safe place to stay until the storm passed. They found a comfortable shelter under a large rock and Penny wrapped her coat around Percy to keep him warm.

As they waited out the storm, Percy looked at Penny with grateful eyes. He realized that their friendship was worth more than any shiny object he could collect. Penny smiled, "Percy, you're my precious friend, and that's all that matters."

When the storm finally subsided, the sun peeked through the clouds, painting the sky with rainbows. Penny and Percy emerged from their shelter, feeling the warmth of the sun on their faces. Penny knew that whatever came their way, she and Percy would face them together.

And so, Penny and Precious Pelican share their days on the beach, collecting seashells, watching the waves and nurturing their unbreakable bond. As the sun set over the horizon, painting the sky orange and pink, their friendship shone like the world's most precious treasure.

the end

19.
"Quincy's Quest for Quills"

Once upon a time, in a green forest, there lived a young porcupine named Quincy. Quincy was a curious and adventurous little hedgehog with a unique dream. He wanted to find the most beautiful and shiny quills to decorate his cozy den.

As you can see, quills are the special spikes that porcupines have on their backs. Quincy's quills were ordinary, but he longed for quills that sparkled like stars. One sunny morning, Quincy decided to set out on a quest to find these remarkable quills.

With his backpack filled with snacks and a map he drew himself, Quincy sets out on his adventure. His best friend, a chatty squirrel named Squeaky, joins him on the journey. "Where are we going, Quincy?" he shouted.

"We're going to find the most amazing quills in the entire forest," Quincy replied excitedly.

As they went deeper into the forest, Quincy and Squawky met all kinds of animals - a wise old owl, a hopping rabbit and even a sleeping turtle. Quincy asked everyone they knew where he could find the shiny quills he was looking for, but no one did.

Feeling a little disappointed, Quincy sat down on a mossy rock. He tried to cheer him up by shouting. "Don't worry, Quincy. We'll find those quills. Maybe we just need to look in the right place." Quincy brightened a bit and decided to ask one more animal before giving up. They find a friendly fox named Felix playing near the crystal-clear stream. Quincy shyly approached him and asked, "Do you know where I can find the shiny quill?"

Felix smiled, "Oh, I know just the place! Follow the stream to the meadow full of colorful flowers. There, you'll find the brightest quills from the meadow birds."

With a renewed sense of hope, Quincy and Squeaky followed the stream and soon reached the meadow. Quincy's eyes widened in surprise as he saw the glittering quills scattered among the flowers. Birds of all colors threw back their wings, and they shone like rainbows.

Quincy carefully collected the quills, making sure not to tear himself. With each quill he picked up, he thanked the birds for sharing their beautiful quills. Squeaky helped him get the quills back to their den.

Back at their den, the Quincy decorates the walls with glowing quills. Her cozy home was transformed into a magical place, filled with colors dancing in the sunlight. Quincy and Squeaky felt proud of their accomplishment.

As the sun set, Quincy looked down at his sparkling hole and said, "Thank you, Squeaky, and thank you, friends of the forest, for helping me find these amazing quills. I may not have made these quills, but I can cherish them and Make my den a colorful masterpiece."

From that day on, Quincy's den became a popular spot in the forest. Animals from all over will visit to marvel at the dazzling quills. Quincy's search for quills brought not only the beauty of his den but also brought him closer to the animals of the forest.

And so, Quincy's search for Quincy becomes a heartwarming story that spreads throughout the forest, reminding everyone that sometimes the most significant treasures are found through friendship, determination, and a bit of sparkle.

And they all lived happily and peacefully.

The End.

20.

"The Secret Song of Sylvia the Sparrow"

Once upon a time, in a cozy little forest, there lived a little sparrow named Sylvia. Sylvia was no ordinary sparrow; He had a secret - a magical song that could bring joy to all who heard it. But Sylvia was shy and hid her song from the world.

Every morning, Sylvia would sit on a branch outside her nest and watch the other birds sing. He wanted to join, but his shyness held him back. One sunny day, as he was listening to the melodious chirping of other birds, he felt a warm breeze whispering through his feathers.

"Sylvia," thought the wind, "your song is special. Let it fly."

Sylvia took a deep breath and parted her lips. At first, only a small peep came out, but as he continued his peep turned into a sweet melody that echoed through the forest. All the animals stopped listening in amazement. The leaves swayed and the flowers grew brighter as Sylvia's magical song filled the air.

When his song reached the ears of the other birds, they felt a wave of joy. Squirrels danced, rabbits jumped, and even the wise old owl was startled. Sylvia's song was like a hug from the heart, wrapping everyone in its warmth.

From that day on, Sylvia's secret song became a daily festival. The animals gathered every morning to listen to his music. Sylvia's shyness melted away, replaced by a new confidence. He befriended blue jays, sparrows, robins and even a curious butterfly named Benny.

One afternoon, when a dark rain cloud covered the sky, Sylvia noticed that the forest was feeling sad. He decided to sing his magical song in hopes of bringing back happiness. As her song flew into the clouds, it transformed into a rainbow that stretched across the sky, painting the world in vibrant colors.
Sylvia's special song spread far and wide. Other forest animals would also come to listen, and even people from nearby villages would travel to listen to his music. Sylvia's song had the power to heal the heart and lift the soul and everyone wanted to feel its magic.
Sylvia's story traveled further afield, reaching the ears of a famous musician. He invites Sylvia to perform at a grand concert in the heart of the village. At first, Sylvia was nervous, but with her friends by her side, she took a deep breath and sang her secret song to the entire crowd.
The magical song fills the hearts of the villagers, making them feel happy and connected. The concert ended with a standing ovation and Sylvia's heart swelled with joy.
From that day Sylvia's secret song became known far and wide. He sings in the forest, sharing his joy with all the animals around him. And whenever anyone felt sad or lonely, they knew they could meet Sylvia and be lifted by her magical melody.
And so, the story of Sylvia, the shy sparrow with a secret song, became a legend, reminding everyone that even the quietest voice can have the power to bring happiness to the world.
And they all lived happily ever after, singing and sharing their joy.
the end

21.
"Ollie's Grand Owl Academy"

Once upon a time, in a magical forest, there lived a young owl named Ollie. Ollie had big, curious eyes and a heart full of dreams. He lived in a cozy nest atop a tall oak tree with his family of owls.

One day, while exploring the forest with his friends, Ollie discovers a mysterious old tree with a sign, "Oli's Grand Owl Academy." Excitement welled up inside him at the thought of what this might mean. Ollie gathered his friends, Flora the Voiceless Falcon, Benny the Brave Bluebird and Sammy the Smart Sparrow, and they all decided to enter the academy.

Inside the tree, they are greeted by an old, wise owl named Professor Hoot. He had a long, white beard and sparkling eyes. Professor Hoot explained that the academy was the place to learn important owl skills such as flying silently, finding food, and even Hoot telling stories!

The first lesson was to fly silently. Professor Hutt demonstrated how to ride through the air without making a sound. Ollie and his friends watched carefully and tried their best to follow. It wasn't easy at first, but with practice and encouragement, they began to improve.

Next, they learned how to find food in the forest. They discovered that rats and insects are their favorite food. They practiced their hunting skills by pretending to catch make-believe prey. It was so much fun, and they were laughing and jumping around.

As the days go by, Ollie and his friends learn many important things about being owls. They learned about different types of trees, how to navigate at night and even how to send instant messages.

One evening, under a starry sky, Professor Hutt gathered everyone around a cozy campfire. He said, "Now, my young owl, it is time to tell your own story." Ollie went ahead and told a story about a brave owl who saved a lost rabbit. Flora shared a story about a falcon and a squirrel who became friends, Benny told a story about a magical blue feather, and Sammy told a funny story about a mischievous mouse.

As their stories filled the air, the forest felt alive with wonder and excitement. Ollie realized that the academy wasn't just about learning skills – it was about sharing stories, making friends and embracing their individuality.

After a long day of learning and laughing, it's time for the graduation ceremony. Ollie and his friends receive special feathers from Professor Hutt, symbolizing their growth and achievement. They knew they would always remember the lessons they learned and the memories they made at Ollie's Grand Owl Academy.

And so, Ollie and his friends return to their forest home with the knowledge and friendship they have gained. They explore, learn and tell stories at night, cherishing the magical moments of their time at the Academy.

And so Ollie's Grand Owl Academy has become a cherished part of the forest, where young owls like Ollie can spread their wings, learn new things, and create stories that will echo through the trees for generations to come.

22.
"Ava and the Enchanted Egret"

Once upon a time, in a peaceful village nestled between rolling hills and a sparkling river, lived a curious and kind girl named Ava. His heart was full of wonder and love for all creatures, especially the beautiful birds that filled the sky.

One sunny morning, as Ava was exploring the meadow near her home, she heard a faint, melodious voice. Following the sound, he stumbled into a clearing where a magnificent egret with snow-white feathers danced gracefully. The egret's feathers seem to shimmer with a magical glow, and its eyes twinkle with a knowing twinkle.

"Hello, beautiful egret!" Ava greeted with a warm smile.

Egret turned her head and nodded in reply, her lips curling into a beautiful smile. "Greetings, Ava," it said in a voice that seemed to echo like a gentle ear.

Ava's eyes widened in surprise. "Can you say?"

"Yes, Ava," answered Egret. "I am Enzo, the enchanted egret. I have the gift of speech, given to me by the ancient magic of our land." Ava's heart raced with excitement. He always dreamed of talking to animals and now, his dream is coming true. "Enzo, it's an honor to meet you! Why are you here dancing alone?"

Enzo sighed softly. "Long ago, the villagers and the animals of this land lived in harmony. But over time, they have forgotten the importance of unity. I dance here hoping that my mesmerizing movement will remind them of the beauty of cooperation and friendship."

Ava nodded in understanding. "I want to help too, Enzo! Let's show everyone we can all get along."

Enzo's eyes brightened even more. "Ava, your soul is as radiant as the morning sun. To achieve our goal, we must gather beings from all around. Each will bring a gift that represents their unique qualities."

And so, Ava and Enzo embark on an adventurous quest. They flew to the top of the tree to meet Oliver the Owl, who shared his wisdom.

They went up the river to meet Finlay the Fish, who offered his fluidity and grace. They even climbed the highest mountain to meet Rosie the Rabbit, who shared her speed.

As the day of the great assembly approached, creatures of all shapes and sizes appeared, each bearing their special gifts. Birds bring music, rabbits bring laughter, and butterflies bring colors that color the sky.

The villagers, mesmerized by the sight, could not help but be impressed by the unity and harmony among the animals. They joined the celebration by realizing the value of working together and embracing their differences.

From that day, the village flourished with new friendships and collaborations. Enzo's fascination with dance, combined with Ava's determination, weaved a bond that would forever bind the villagers and the animals of the land.

As time passes, Ava continues to visit Enzo, sharing stories of their adventures and enjoying the beauty of their unbreakable friendship. And every time he looked up at the sky and saw a graceful egret in flight, he remembered the magic of unity that had transformed his village and his life.

And so, the story of Ava and the Enchanted Egret became a timeless tale, reminding everyone that when hearts come together, they can create harmony as bright as the sunlit sky.

the end

23.
"Pippin's Penguin Pal"

Once upon a time, in a land of ice and snow, there lived a little penguin named Pippin. Pippin loved to slide on the ice, catch fish and play with his other penguin friends. But there was something special about Pippin – he had a big heart and always wanted to make new friends.

One cold morning, as Pippin was walking by the sea, he heard a strange noise. It was a soft, mournful chirp from a small cave near the ice bank. Pippin, curious and kind, followed the word. Inside the cave, he found a baby seagull alone.

Pippin approached the baby seagull gently and said, "Hello dear! My name is Pippin. What's your name?" The baby seagull looked up with big, watery eyes and said, "I'm Pip. I've lost my way from my seagull family and now I'm all alone."

Sorry about Pippin Pip. He knew what it was like to be alone, so he decided to help. "Don't worry, Pip. You're not alone anymore. You can be my penguin pal!" cried Pippin.

From that day on, Pippin and Pip become best friends. They did everything together. They slide down icy mountains, play tag with other penguins, and even go fishing side by side. Pip was not as good at fishing as Pippin, but Pippin showed him how to dive into the water and catch tasty fish.

Their friendship grows stronger day by day. Pippin introduces Pip to all his penguin friends, and soon, Pip has a whole group of new friends. The penguins loved Pip's seagull stories and his laughter that sounded like gentle waves.

One sunny day, as Pippin and Pip were building a sandcastle on the snowy shore, they heard a familiar squawk. It was Pip's seagull family! They were looking for Pip all along. Pip was excited but a little sad. He didn't want to leave his penguin pal Pippin.

Pippin finds that Pip is torn between his old family and his new friend. Smiling, Pippin said, "Pip, you should go back to your family. They miss you so much, and I will, too. But friends want the best for each other, and I want you to be happy."

Pip hugged Pippin tightly. "Thank you, Pippin, for being my best friend," Pip said with happy tears in his eyes.

Pippin waved and smiled as Pip flew away with his family of seagulls. She knew that even though Pip was gone, their friendship would always be in her heart.

And so, Pippin continued to slide on the ice, catch fish and play with his penguin friends. He often looked up at the sky and thought about his brave and special penguin pal Pip. And whenever he saw seagulls flying overhead, he knew that somewhere up there was a little seagull that would always be his friend.

And it's the heartwarming story of Pippin's penguin flock, a story of friendship, kindness and the joy of making new friends, no matter how different they are.

24.
"Tiki and the Tropical Treasures"

Once upon a time, on a distant island surrounded by a sparkling blue sea, there lived a colorful parrot named Tiki. Tiki had vibrant feathers that looked like rainbows and loved to explore the lush forests and sandy shores of her island home.

One sunny morning, as Tiki was playing in a coconut tree, she heard a soft, mysterious whisper. "Follow the waving palm, dear Tiki, and you'll find treasure beyond your wildest dreams," said the wind. Tiki's curious heart fluttered with excitement. He had heard stories of treasures, and now he wanted to find them.

Gathering his courage, Tiki spread his wings and flew away. He followed the path of swaying palms, flying over turquoise water and dense jungle, until he reached a hidden waterfall. Behind the waterfall, Tiki discovered a secret cave covered in glittering gems and bright gold coins. He found the tropical treasure!

As Tiki explores the cave, she finds a glittering necklace with a sparkling pendant. He carefully lifted it with his lips, and as soon as he did, the pendant glowed brightly and a kind voice echoed in the cave. "Greetings, young adventurer! You have unlocked the magic of these treasures. They are for those who use them for good."

Tiki's heart warmed as she realized that these treasures were not meant to be hoarded, but to bring joy to others. He thought of his friends on the island and how these treasures could help them.

With the magical pendant around her neck, Tiki returned to her island home. He gathered his friends - the mischievous monkey, the wise old turtle and the playful dolphin - and showed them the treasure. As the pendant brightened, Tiki wished the island would bloom with more colorful flowers and abundant fruits.

The island was transformed before their eyes, and everyone cheered for joy. Monkeys were happily swinging from the trees, turtles were slow dancing, and dolphins were jumping for joy in the ocean waves.

Tiki and his friends decided to use the treasure to help not only their island, but also the surrounding ocean and other animals. The pendant had the power to heal coral reefs, bring rain to dry lands, and even repair the broken wings of injured birds.

From that day on, Tiki and his friends became the guardians of tropical treasures. They shared the magic of wealth with all creatures of land and sea, making their island paradise a haven of happiness and harmony.

And so, Tiki the colorful parrot learns that the true value of riches lies not in gold and gems, but in the happiness they bring when shared with a caring heart. And he lived happily, flying high in the sky and spreading kindness wherever he went.

the end

25.

"The Feathered Friends' Festival"

Once upon a time, a group of colorful and cheerful birds lived in the bosom of the magical forest. They were known far and wide as Feathered Friends. These birds were not just ordinary birds; They were special because they loved to celebrate and spread joy.

One sunny morning, the feathered friends gathered in a cozy clearing as the first rays of light peeked through the trees. It was a day they had been eagerly waiting for—Feathered Friends Festival! Every year, they organize this grand festival to bring joy and laughter to the entire forest.

Among the feathered friends were Ruby the Robin with her bright red breast, Freddy the Finch with her cheerful chirping and Polly the Parrot with her rainbow feathers. There were many more, each with its own unique color and song.

The festival was full of colors and laughter. The trees were decorated with colorful ribbons and the ground was covered with petals of all colors. The birds worked together to create the most beautiful decoration. There were small lanterns hanging from the branches and garlands of delicate flowers fluttering in the wind.

As the sun rises high in the sky, the feathered friends start the festival with a grand parade. They flew through the forest, singing their melodious tunes and flapping their wings. Other forest animals also joined in, dancing and clapping their hands. Even the butterflies came to watch, mesmerized by the magical sight.

After the parade, it was time for games and competitions. There was the Great Nest Building Contest, where groups of birds worked together to build strong nests. Ruby Robin's team won this year, and their nest was so cozy that everyone wanted to sleep in it!

Next came the whistling wind race, where the birds had to fly against the wind and reach the finish line first. Freddy the Finch won with his swift wings and joyful spirit. The crowd cheered and clapped, their excitement filling the air.

But the highlight of the festival was Polly the Parrot's talent show. Birds around the forest display their amazing talents. Some sang sweetly like honey, while others danced gracefully in the sky. Polly himself surprised everyone with his ability to imitate the sounds of other animals. He brings the forest to life with his playful performances.

As the day turned to evening, the feathered friends gathered around a bonfire. They shared stories, sang songs, and laughed until they had feathers. It was a day filled with happiness, friendship and forest magic.

As the festivities ended, the feathered friends felt a deep sense of satisfaction. They not only celebrated their own happiness but also spread happiness to everyone around them. The forest animals went to sleep that night with smiles on their faces, dreaming of the next feast of feathered friends.

And so, year after year, the feathered friends continued to organize their wonderful festival, reminding everyone that the simple joy of coming together, celebrating and making others happy was the most magical thing.

26.
"Finley's Feathered Fables"

Once upon a time in an enchanted forest lived a young blue jay named Finley. Finlay was known far and wide for his colorful feathers and his excellent storytelling. Every evening, all the birds and animals would gather around a cozy tree stump to listen to Finley's charming stories.

One sunny morning, as Finlay sits on a branch, he notices a sad-looking sparrow named Sophie sitting alone. Curious, he jumped up and asked, "Hello, Sophie! Why the long face?"

Sophie sighed and replied, "I wish I could fly as high as you and tell stories like you, Finley."

Finley smiled kindly, "Well, Sophie, how can I teach you to tell your own story? You have your own special voice!"

Sophie's eyes lit up with excitement. "Really? But I don't know where to start."

"Don't worry," Finley said, "I'll show you the way. We'll call them 'Feathered Fables."

And so, every day after their morning song, Finlay and Sophie would sit under the wise old oak tree and Finlay would share his storytelling secrets.

"First," Finlay began, "imagine a world where animals talk and have exciting adventures. Think of a hero, a challenge, and a lesson."

Sophie nodded eagerly. "Like a brave squirrel who finds lost treasure?"

"Right!" Finley shouted. "Now, add some magic, like talking trees or flying butterflies."

As the days turned into weeks, Sophie's confidence grew. He started telling stories about squirrels that sang sweet songs and rivers that told secrets to the wind. Everyone loved his stories, and couldn't wait to gather every evening to hear them.

One day a shy rabbit named Rosie came to Sophie. "Your stories make me so happy," Rosie said. "Can you teach me to tell feathered tales too?"

Under Finley's guidance, Sophie taught Rosie how to create magic. Soon, more animals join in, and they form a storytelling club under the oak tree. Each member has added their own twist to the story, making it even more mesmerizing.

One evening, as the sun set and the stars began to twinkle, Finlay felt a warmth in his heart. She realized that her feather fiction not only brought joy but also inspired others to find their voice. The animals continued to gather, sharing their stories and the forest echoed with laughter and wonder. And as for Finley, he was the proudest blue jay in the entire forest, knowing that his kindness helped create a community of storytellers.

And so, dear friends, the feathered fables of the forest continue to be told by birds and animals alike, reminding us all that our unique voices and stories make the world a more magical place.

And remember, like Finlay, you too have the power to share your own wonderful stories with the world.

the end

27.
"Sasha and the Sky Serenade"

Once upon a time in a land of fluffy clouds and bright blue skies, there lived a little sparrow named Sasha. Sasha had the most beautiful voice of all the birds in his forest. Every morning, he would wake up and sing his sweet melody, filling the air with joy and happiness.

Sasha loved watching the sunrise from her favorite branch. One morning, as the first rays of sunlight peeked over the horizon, Sasha began to sing her heart out. Her melodious melody echoed through the trees, attracting the attention of all the forest animals.

But there was someone special who was listening from afar. It was Skyler, a graceful eagle with majestic wings. Skyler was known for his great flight and his love of music. He had heard stories of Sasha's enchanting singing and had always wanted to meet her.

One day, as Sasha was singing her morning song, she noticed a large shadow hovering over her. He looked up and saw Skyler, the eagle, gliding elegantly in the sky. Sasha's heart trembled with excitement. Skyler landed softly on a branch next to Sasha. "Congratulations, Sasha! Your song is as beautiful as the whisper of the wind. Will you join me in a musical duet? Let's create a melody that will be heard throughout the forest," Skyler suggested with a friendly smile. Sasha was thrilled beyond words. He nodded eagerly and replied, "Oh, Skyler, I'd be honored to sing with you!"

As the sun sets, painting the sky with oranges and pinks, Sasha and Skyler begin their duet. Sasha's delicate notes meld harmoniously with Skyler's powerful vocals. The forest stood still, enchanted by the magical serenade echoing through the trees.

Animals gathered from all around to listen to the mesmerizing music. Squirrels, rabbits, and even a curious deer joined the visitors. Sasha and Skyler's voices rose, their tones carried far.

As the last note faded into the evening air, the forest erupted in cheers and applause. Sasha and Skyler took a bow, their hearts full of joy. They created a melody that united the creatures of the forest in a way they had never experienced before.

From that day on, Sasha and Skyler became best friends. They were often seen at sunrise and sunset singing their celestial serenades, sharing their love of music and friendship. Their duets continue to bring happiness to the forest, reminding everyone that when different voices come together, they create something truly magical.

And so, Sasha and Skyler's songs can still be heard every morning and evening, a testament to the power of harmony and the beauty of friendship that rose as high as the sky.

28.
"Finn's Flap-tastic Adventure"

Once upon a time, in a colorful and bustling forest, there lived a young blue jay named Finn. Finn was known for his boundless energy and his love for soaring. Every day, he would see clouds and dream of exciting adventures.

One sunny morning, Finn wakes up with an idea that will change his life forever. "I'm going on a flap-tastic adventure today!" She chirped excitedly. Packing a small backpack with some snacks, he set off.

Finn's first stop was at the river bank, where he saw a group of ducks frolicking around. "Hello there!" One of the ducks quacked. "Would you like to join us?"

Finn hesitated for a moment, then said firmly, "I'm on an adventure today! But maybe we can run to that big oak tree on the other side?" The duck agreed, and with a loud "quack!" They were closed. Finn flapped his wings with all his might, and although he wasn't as swift as a duck on water, he kept a positive attitude. When they reached the oak tree, the duck congratulated Finn on his efforts and he felt proud of himself.

Next, Finn comes across a family of squirrels gathering acorns. "Hey, Finn! Want to help us find the juiciest acorn?" asked Sammy, the friendly squirrel.

Finn smiled and replied, "I'd love to, Sammy! But I'm on an adventure, and I've got to flap my wings. How about a flying race to the top of that mountain?"

The squirrels agreed and left. Finn soared upward, feeling the air rush through his feathers. He reached the top shortly after the squirrels, but they all cheered for him, impressed by his determination.

As the day goes on, Finn encounters a group of butterflies near a field of wildflowers. "Hello, Finn!" A butterfly greeted. "Care to dance with us?"

Finn laughed happily. "I love to dance, but I'm on a flap-tastic adventure today! How about a flying and spinning race around those trees?"

The butterflies agreed, and they fluttered around in the air as Finn jumped alongside them. Although he couldn't spin as elegantly as a butterfly, he added his own flair to running. When they finished, the butterflies admired Finn's creativity and he felt even more inspired. As the sun began to set, Finn realized his adventure was coming to an end. He went back to his nest with happiness and sharing of stories. "Today was really flap-delicious!" He chirped to his family. From that day on, Finn became a well-known adventurer in the forest. He learns that while he may not be the fastest, most skilled, or fancy, his drive and determination make his adventure truly special.

And so, Blue Jay who once dreamed of flying in the clouds discovered that every flap of his wings brought him to the magic of the world around him. And that, my dear friends, is the story of Finn's flap-tastic adventure - the adventure that showed him the true meaning of flying with a heart.

29.
"Polly's Pirate Parrot Puzzle"

Once upon a time on a sunny island, there lived a little parrot named Polly. He had bright green feathers and an inquisitive mind. Polly loved exploring the island and meeting new friends. One day, while jumping from tree to tree, he hears a rumor about hidden pirate treasure!

Polly's wings fluttered in excitement at the thought of the treasure. He decided to start an adventure to find it. But to reach the treasure he had to solve a puzzle. Polly was not afraid; He loved solving puzzles.

Polly begins her journey, flying over colorful forests and sandy beaches. Along the way, he meets his friends, Sammy the Squirrel and Benny the Bunny. They join him, excited for the adventure.

As they explore, they find an old, torn map with strange markings. "It must be the puzzle mentioned on the map," exclaimed Polly. Benny and Sammy agree, and they study the map together. The first clue led them to the tallest palm tree on the island. Polly saw a message carved into the buckle: "Three steps to the left, and you'll find the key." Polly, Benny and Sammy count their steps and find a shiny golden key hidden under the leaves. With the key in her lips, Polly led her friends deeper into the island. Following the next clue they reached a sparkling waterfall. Behind the waterfall, they discovered a hidden cave. The cave was filled with colorful shells and in the middle they found a locked chest. Polly tried on the gold key, and to their delight, it fit perfectly. The chest opened, revealing a sparkling necklace with a sparkling gem. "Wow, that's beautiful!" Sammy exclaimed. But there was one last clue: "To the highest mountain, you must go, and there the ultimate treasure will burn." Polly, Benny, and Sammy climb the highest mountain, where they see a bright rainbow in the sky. At the end of the rainbow, they find a box filled with gold coins and precious gems. Polly, Benny and Sammy cheer with joy! They solved the pirate parrot puzzle and found the treasure. The island was alive with their laughter and excitement. Polly shared the treasure with all her friends on the island, and they had a great feast together. Sparkling necklaces, gold coins and jewels became reminders of their incredible adventures. From that day on, Polly, Benny and Sammy became known as the island's most daring adventurers. They discovered that solving puzzles with friends made the journey more special. And so, the story of Polly's pirate parrot puzzle spreads across the island, inspiring others to go on exciting adventures and make new friends. And whenever anyone needed a little courage, they looked up to the sky and remembered the parrots who found the treasure through teamwork and curiosity.

And they all lived happily ever after.

The End

30.
"Lulu's Lost Lark"

Once upon a time, there lived a little girl named Lulu in a land filled with green forests and sparkling blue lakes. Lulu was a curious and kind girl who loved to spend her days exploring the beauty of nature. But his favorite was the sweet song of the birds that filled the air.

Lulu had a special bond with a tiny, cheerful lark named Lola. Lola was no ordinary lark; His feathers glittered like gold in the sunlight, and his voice could lift the spirits of anyone who heard it. Every morning, Lulu would wake up to the sound of Lola's enchanting song. They will play hide and seek among the trees and dance in the meadow, sharing their joys and secrets.

One sunny morning, Lulu wakes up excited to meet Lola during their usual playtime. He ran to where they usually met, but there was no sign of Lola. Lulu looked around, calling his name, but the forest remained silent. Panic started to grow in the mind. "Where could Lola be?" Lulu said in surprise.

Lulu decides to search everywhere for Lola. He explored the tallest trees, peered under rocks and even called her to the shimmering lake. But Lola was nowhere to be found. Lulu's worry turned to sadness, and she sat down by a babbling brook, tears rolling down her eyes.

Just then, a wise old owl named Oliver calls softly from a nearby branch. "Why do you look so sad, young Lulu?" he asked.

Lulu wipes her tears and tells Oliver about Lola's disappearance. Oliver listened intently, then rolled his wise eyes and said, "Don't despair, dear Lulu. Sometimes, even the brightest stars take a moment to shine again. Remember, friends find their way back to each other."

Feeling a glimmer of hope, Lulu decides to follow Oliver's advice. He built a small nest of leaves and twigs near the spot where he and Lola used to meet. Every morning and evening, he sang sweet songs that they sang together, hoping that Lola would hear and find her way back.

Days turned into weeks, and Lulu's determination never wavered. Then, one magical morning, as Lulu sang a familiar tune, a soft, golden melody joined her. Lulu's heart skips a beat when she turns to see Lola sitting on a branch, her feathers shining in the sunlight.

"Lola! You're back!" Lulu exclaimed, her eyes shining with joy.

Lola chirped happily and flew down to rest on Lulu's shoulder. He told Lulu about his adventures, how he followed a beautiful rainbow that led him to distant lands and new friends. But in her heart, she knew that her true friend, Lulu, was where she really belonged.

From that day on, Lulu and Lola were inseparable again. They sing, dance and play, their bond stronger than ever. And whenever they sang their song, the whole forest joined in, creating a symphony of joy that echoed across the land.

And so, the story of Lulu and Lola teaches everyone that even when friends are separated, their bond remains strong. Like Lola's golden melody, friendship always finds a way to brighten our lives, filling them with love and happiness.

And they all lived happily, chirping and singing, in a land of green forests and sparkling blue lakes.

the end

31.
"Feathers and Friends: The Great Avian Adventure"

Once upon a time in a colorful forest lived a group of happy and playful birds. They came from different parts of the world and became best friends. There was Ruby the Red Cardinal, Sunny the Yellow Finch, Bluey the Blue Jay and more.

One sunny morning, while the birds were chirping, they noticed something unusual. A shiny object fell from the sky and landed near their favorite tree. It was a mysterious map with a picture of a treasure. The friends chatted around the map, excited about the adventure ahead.

"We should follow this map and find the treasure," Ruby shouted, her red feathers burning with excitement.

Sunny nodded, her yellow feathers glowing brightly. "That sounds like a fun avian adventure! Let's do it together."

With hearts full of excitement, the feathered friends spread their wings and set off. The map took them through thick forests, sparkling rivers and high mountains. Along the way, they faced challenges like strong winds and tricky puzzles, but their friendship and tenacity helped them overcome every obstacle.

As they flew, the friends discovered new places they had never seen before. They marveled at the beauty of nature and shared stories of their own homes. Bluey, the blue jay, told tales of the vast sky, while Polly the parrot shared tales of far-off jungles.

After flying for days, the friends finally reached the location marked on the map. They found themselves in front of a magnificent waterfall that sparkled like a diamond in the sunlight. As they approached, they saw something hidden behind the waterfall—a house made of gold and jewels!

Gasping in amazement, the birds realized that the real treasure was the journey itself and the wonderful memories they created together. They laughed, they sang, and they danced around the sparkling waterfall, feeling like the luckiest birds in the world.

With their hearts full of joy, the friends decide to keep the treasure a secret, allowing it to remain as a special memory shared only between them. Cherishing the bond they had formed and the incredible adventure they had experienced, they retraced their journey back home.

And so, the birds returned to their colorful forest, where they continued to play, explore and share stories. The map remains in their tree as a reminder of the amazing adventure that brought them closer as friends. And whenever they looked at it, they couldn't help but smile, knowing that they were part of something truly special—the great avian adventure that filled their hearts with joy.

32.
"Sunny the Singing Sparrow's Spectacular Surprise"

Once upon a time, in a cozy little forest, there lived a sparrow named Sunny. Sunny was no ordinary sparrow - she had the most beautiful and melodious voice. Every morning, he would sit on a branch and sing his heart out, filling the forest with his sweet melody.

Other animals in the forest loved listening to Sunny's music. Rabbits, squirrels and even wise old owls will gather around to listen to her sing. Sunny's music brought joy to everyone and his songs became the soundtrack of the forest.

One day, while Sunny was practicing a new song, she heard a singing competition that was going to be held in a nearby meadow. The surrounding animals were going to participate and the winner would receive a shiny gold feather as a prize. Sunny was excited but nervous. He had never sung in front of so many animals before.

With determination in his heart, Sunny decided to join the competition. He practiced day and night, pouring his heart and soul into his songs. His forest friends cheered him on and encouraged him to believe in himself.

Finally the day of the competition arrived. The meadow was filled with animals of all shapes and sizes. Sunny felt her wings tremble with stage fright, but she took a deep breath and flew onto the stage.

When he began to sing, the whole meadow fell silent. Sunny's voice was so beautiful it was coloring the air.

When he sang, the animals couldn't help but be mesmerized by his voice. The judges smiled and nodded in agreement. As Sunny finished her performance, the meadow erupted into applause. Even the flowers are swaying to the rhythm of his music.

The judges announced the winner, and to everyone's delight, it was Sunny the Singing Sparrow! He was given a glittering golden feather, and his forest friends cheered with joy. Sunny's surprise was truly spectacular, and she realized that believing in herself and sharing her gift led to this wonderful moment.

Since that day, Sunny continued to sing in the forest, but now he also goes to the neighboring meadows and shares his songs with other animals. He became an inspiration to all, showing that with courage and determination anyone can achieve their dreams.

And so, the forest and beyond was filled with the melodious tunes of Sunny the Singing Sparrow, reminding everyone that even the smallest among us can create the most spectacular surprises.

And they all lived harmoniously.

33.
"Piper's Perch: A Tale of Courage and Friendship"

Once upon a time, in a lively forest, there lived a little blue bird named Piper. Piper was smaller than the other birds, but she had a big heart and loved to sing. He had a cozy nest in a tall tree, which he called his perch.

One sunny morning, while Piper was practicing her cheerful song, she noticed a group of birds gathered near a large, scary bush.

Curious, he flew to see what was happening. There he saw a little bird named Rosie stuck in a thorn in a bush. Rosie was a timid bird who often felt nervous about new things.

Without hesitation, Piper reached down and tried to help Rosie. With her delicate lips she carefully plucked her feather from the

thorn. It took time and patience, but Piper never gave up. He spoke calmly to Rosie, telling her that everything would be alright. As the piper works, the other birds join in to help. Some use their hard beaks to gently widen the thorny gaps, while others bring tender leaves for Rosie to land on. Together, they managed to free Rosie from the bush. He was scared and shaking, but safe. Rosie looked at Piper with grateful eyes. He had never experienced such generosity and bravery before. Piper smiled a warm smile, "You're safe now, Rosie. Friends help each other."
From that day on, Piper and Rosie became best friends. They sang together, shared stories and encouraged each other to try new things. Rosie's confidence grows, and Piper's courage inspires everyone in the forest.
One stormy day, as the wind howled and the rain poured down, Piper noticed a nest in a nearby tree about to fall. Without a second's thought he flew through the storm towards the endangered nest. Rosie followed behind. With their combined efforts, they were able to secure the nest, saving the baby birds inside.
The forest animals watched Piper and Rosie's act of courage and friendship. They all cheered and chirped in appreciation. Piper and Rosie not only saved the nest, but also showed everyone the power of kindness and unity.
In time, stories of Piper and Rosie's adventures spread throughout the forest. They become legends, and their names are mentioned with respect and admiration.
And so, in the heart of the vibrant forest, two little birds showed everyone that even small acts of courage and friendship can make a big difference. The piper's perch became a symbol of hope and unity, reminding all creatures that they were stronger when they united.
And they all lived forever.

34.
"Oliver Owl's Enchanted Moonlit Flight"

Once upon a time, in a peaceful forest, there lived an owl named Oliver. Oliver was different from other owls - he was curious and adventurous. He loved to explore the forest and learn about the world around him.

On a clear night, as the full moon shines brightly in the sky, Oliver feels a strange tingling in his feathers. He heard stories from his owl friends about magical moonlight flights that happened once in a lifetime. Owls can experience something extraordinary during this flight.

Excited and a little nervous, Oliver spread his wings and flew into the night sky. He felt the gentle breeze beneath his wings as he soared higher. The silver light of the moon surrounded him, making everything enchanting.

As Oliver flew, he noticed something sparkling in the distance. It was a path of twinkling stars leading to a hidden part of the forest he had never explored before. Curiosity got the better of him, and he followed the star's path.

The path led Oliver to a clearing where a group of fireflies danced in harmony. Their soft glow illuminates the area, creating a magical atmosphere. Oliver watched in amazement, feeling as if he had entered a dream world.

Among the fireflies, Oliver notices a wise old owl named Luna. Luna had kind eyes that twinkled like stars. He explained that the enchanted moonlight was an opportunity for the owls to connect with the magic of the night and learn from the creatures attuned to it.

Luna taught Oliver the importance of balance in nature and how each animal plays its role. He talks about the beauty of the night, its secrets and the stories it whispers to those who listen.

After a heartwarming conversation, Oliver knew it was time to return to his forest home. Luna smiled and told him that the magic of moonlight flight would always be a part of him, guiding him to make wise choices and cherish the world around him.

With a grateful heart and new knowledge, Oliver spread his wings and returned home. The forest looked different now - more alive and connected. Oliver knew he would always remember this magical night and the important lessons he learned.

From that day on, Oliver Owl became known as a wise and caring friend to all the animals in the forest. And whenever the moon shone brightly, he would look and remember his enchanted moon flight, which he carried forever in his heart.

And so, in the heart of the forest, Oliver's story becomes a legend, inspiring generations of owls to embrace their individuality and always seek the magic of the night.

the end

35.
"Peep and Tweet: The Little Birds Who Saved the Day"

Once upon a time in a colorful and vibrant forest lived two little birds named Pip and Tweet. They were best friends and did everything together. Pip was a small and brave blue bird, while Tweet was a cute and chatty yellow canary.

One sunny morning, as Pip and Tweet were playing near their nest, they heard worried whispers among the forest animals. "The big storm is coming!" squeaked the rat. "Oh no, our houses will be destroyed!" The wise old owl hoots.

Pip and Tweet looked up at the dark clouds gathering in the sky. They knew they had to do something to help their friends. "We may be small, but we can make a big difference," Pip exclaims optimistically.

Two small birds quickly flew into action. Pip used his strong beak to gather twigs, while Tweety used his nimble feet to gather leaves and grass. They built a strong shelter near the forest floor, a safe haven for rats and rabbits.

As the storm came, the rain poured down and the wind howled. Pip and Tweet's shelter was strong, protecting their friends from the angry weather. The forest animals huddled inside, grateful for the quick thinking and hard work of the little birds.

But the storm was not over yet. The river is beginning to rise, and the beavers are in trouble. Without hesitation Pip and Tweet flew to the river. They found large leaves and pieces of bark to make rafts. Through their teamwork, they helped the beavers reach higher ground, saving them from the swift water.

News of Pip and Tweet's adventure spread throughout the forest. The animals saw that even the smallest creatures could have a huge impact. The storm finally passed and the sun began to shine again. The animals of the forest gathered to thank Pip and Tweet for their courage and kindness. "You may be small, but your heart is as big as the sky," said the wise old owl. From that day on, Pip and Tweet were known as the heroes of the forest.

And so, Pip and Tweet's friendship and bravery inspired everyone in the forest. They show that with determination and teamwork, even the smallest creatures can save the day and make a world of difference. And as the sun set over the colorful forest, the two little birds knew that true friendship and kindness can conquer any challenge.

And this is the heartwarming story of Pip and Tweet, the little birds who saved the day

36.
"Rainbow Feathers: The Magical Journey of Skyler the Parrot"

Once upon a time there lived a parrot named Skylar in a colorful forest. Skylar was not like other parrots; She had beautiful feathers that were as bright as a rainbow. Every color you can imagine was present in his feathers. But what made Skylar truly special was her dream of exploring the world beyond the jungle.

One sunny morning, while the jungle birds were singing and the leaves were rustling, Skyler shared her dream with her best friend, the mango monkey. Mango loved Skyler's colorful feathers and believed that Skyler's dreams could come true. "You can do it, Skyler!" Mango encouraged.

With determination in her heart, Skyler begins her adventure. He flew into the sky, feeling the wind beneath his rainbow wings. He visited meadows, mountains and rivers, making friends with all kinds of animals. Skyler's vibrant plumage caught everyone's attention and brought smiles wherever she flew.

But the journey was not always easy. Skylar faced challenges like stormy weather and unfamiliar places. Still, he never gave up. He remembered the wise words of his friend Mango and continued to learn to face each obstacle.

One day, while sitting in a tall tree, Skyler sees a shimmering lake in the distance. He felt attracted to it and flew closer. As soon as he reached the lake, some miracle happened. Skyler's rainbow feathers reflect on the water, creating a breathtaking display of colors dancing on the surface.

Amazed by this sight, other birds gathered around the lake to witness the scene. Skyler's rainbow feathers brought them together in a way she never imagined. He realized that his uniqueness could bring joy and unity to all those around him.

With a heart full of joy, Skyler decides to return to her forest home. When he returned, he took with him the lessons of his journey—the importance of following your dreams, facing challenges with courage, and embracing what makes you special.

When she returns to the forest, Skyler is greeted by Mango and all her friends. He shared with them his adventures and stories of the magical lake. Since that day, Skyler's rainbow feathers have not only shone brightly in the sky; They also brightened the spirits of everyone they met.

And so, Skyler the parrot lived happily ever after, surrounded by friends who cherished his vibrant feathers and the colorful lessons he brought back from his magical journeys.

the end

37.
"Flutter's First Flight: A Hummingbird's Big Dream"

Once upon a time there lived a small hummingbird named Flutter in a colorful garden. Flutter was a curious and adventurous bird, but there was one thing he dreamed of more than anything else: flying high in the sky.

Every day, the other birds watched in awe as Flutter flew through the air. He will flap his wings and try to lift, but he always hovers just above the ground. "I wish I could fly like them," Flutter sighed.

One sunny morning, Flutter's friend the Ruby Butterfly casts her longing gaze into the sky. "Why the long face, Flutter?" Ruby asked. "I want to fly in the sky like other birds," replied Flutter. "But every time I try, I just can't go up."

Ruby smiled softly. "Flutter, you're a hummingbird! Your wings are special. They beat so fast they make a magical buzz. You just have to believe in yourself."

Encouraged by Ruby's words, Fluttershy decided to try again. He flapped his little wings faster than ever. Suddenly, he felt a tingle of excitement as he began to rise into the air. He went higher, and for the first time, he was flying between trees and clouds.

As Flutter grows, he realizes that flying isn't as easy as he thought. The wind was strong, and he had to use all his strength to stay still. But he did not give up. He remembered Ruby's advice and believed in himself.

Over time, Flutter's wings grow stronger and she becomes more adept at flying. He zipped through the garden, sipping nectar from flowers and making new friends along the way. He even had friendly runs with other birds and they marveled at his incredible speed.

One day, as the sun was setting, Flutter found himself walking towards the tallest tree in the garden. He sat on a branch and looked down at the world below. He realized that his big dream had come true. He was a hummingbird that could fly in the sky!
From that day on, Flutterstered outside the garden to explore the sky and the earth. He never forgot the lesson he learned: that with determination and confidence, even the tiniest of birds can achieve their biggest dreams.
And so, Flutter's first flight became a legend in the garden, inspiring all creatures to pursue their dreams, no matter how big or small they were.
And they all lived happily and bravely.

38.
"Robbie the Robin's Remarkable Resilience"

Once upon a time, in a cozy little nest in a tree, lived Robbie the Robin and his family. Robbie was a small and curious robin with bright red feathers on his chest.
One day, as the sun rose in the sky, Ravi and his siblings stepped out of their home for the first time. They flapped their wings and felt the cool breeze ruffle their feathers. Ravi was excited to explore the world.
As days go by, Ravi and his siblings learn to fly better and higher. They practiced landing on branches and even learned to catch bugs for their food. But one stormy day, dark clouds covered the sky and a strong wind started blowing.
Ravi's siblings quickly retreated to the safety of their nest, but Ravi was trapped by a gust of wind. He struggles to stay in the air, his feathers drenched by the rain. A sudden gust of wind caused him to lose his balance and fall into the bush.
Ravi gets scared and injured. His wings weren't moving like he should, and he felt intense pain. He remained in the bush, unable to

fly or move. But Robbie was a determined Robin. He remembered what his parents had taught him about never giving up.

The day passed, and Ravi remained in the bush, resting and slowly trying to move his wings. He saw other birds flying, and he felt jealous. But he did not lose hope. She uses her lips to groom her feathers as best she can.

One sunny morning, a kind sparrow named Sammy notices Ravi in the bushes. Sammy saw Robbie practicing flying before the storm and wondered what happened to him. Sammy jumped up and chirped, "Hey Robbie, you okay?"

Robbie explained his situation to Sammy, and Sammy nodded sympathetically. "Don't worry, Robbie. I'll help you," Sammy said. He brought some soft leaves and twigs and together they built a small, cozy nest in the bush.

With Sammy's help, Robbie's days become more bearable. They talked about their favorite flying stories, and Robbie felt a little better every day. He rested and continued to exercise his wings, never losing his aim to fly again.

Weeks passed, and Robbie's wing slowly recovered. He practiced flapping it slowly and then with more force. Sammy cheered him on, and Robbie's resolve grew stronger. Finally, the day came when Ravi felt his wings were ready.

With a deep breath and a leap of faith, Ravi pushed off the ground and flapped his wings with all his might. He wobbles at first but then flies into the air, higher. Ravi flew again!

Other birds in the area chirped with joy at Ravi's triumphant flight. Ravi realized that his resilience had paid off, and he was back where he belonged - among the birds of the sky.

From that day on, Robbie the Robin became known for his extraordinary resilience. He knew that no matter how difficult things came, he could overcome them with determination and the support of friends like Sammy.

And so, Ravi's story has spread far and wide, inspiring birds of all kinds to never give up on their dreams, no matter what challenges come their way.